Pandas

Debbie Gallagher

 **Marshall Cavendish**
Benchmark
New York

Library of Congress Cataloging-in-Publication Data

Gallagher, Debbie, 1969–
    Pandas / Debbie Gallagher.
      p. cm. — (Zoo animals)
    Summary: "Discusses pandas, their natural habitat,
    behavior, and
    characteristics, and zoo life"—Provided by publisher.
    Includes index.
    ISBN 978-0-7614-4745-0
    1. Pandas—Juvenile literature. I. Title.
    QL737.C27G35 2010
    599.789—dc22
                                        2009040079

First published in 2010 by
MACMILLAN EDUCATION AUSTRALIA PTY LTD
15–19 Claremont Street, South Yarra 3141

Visit our website at www.macmillan.com.au or go directly to
www.macmillanlibrary.com.au

Associated companies and representatives throughout the
world.

Copyright © Debbie Gallagher 2010

Edited by Georgina Garner
Text and cover design by Kerri Wilson
Page layout by Raul Diche
Photo research by Legend Images
Base maps by Gaston Vanzet, modified by Kerri Wilson

Printed in the United States

Acknowledgments
The author and the publisher are grateful to the following for
permission to reproduce copyright material:

Front cover photo of pair of 8-month old pandas at Wolong
Nature Reserve, China © Frank Lukasseck/Corbis

Photographs courtesy of: © Frank Lukasseck/Corbis, 1; © Li
Wen/Xinhua Press/Corbis, 21; Monika Fiby, 29; © Meredith
Blache/iStockphoto, 13; © Terri Kieffer/iStockphoto, 22; © rest/
iStockphoto, 10; Legendimages, 3, 7, 20, 24, 25, 26 (left);
© Newspix/AFP PHOTO/HO/Ken BOHN/SAN DIEGO ZOO,
27 (left); © Newspix/News Ltd/Nathan Edwards, 26 (right);
Photolibrary © Nature/Alamy, 5; Photolibrary/Eric Baccega,
6, 16; Photolibrary/Corbis, 14; Photolibrary/Fritz Polking, 11;
Connie Shea, 19; © Mike Flippo/Shutterstock, 15; © Brian L.
Hendricks/Shutterstock, 12; © Johny Keny/Shutterstock, 30;
© Glenda M. Powers/Shutterstock, 4; © Sneza/Shutterstock, 8
(giant panda silhouette); © Ismael Montero Verdu/Shutterstock,
8 (red panda silhouette); Taronga Zoo/Rick Stevens, 27
(right);Miles Wu (copyright 2007), 28; Zoo Atlanta, 17, 18; Zoos
SA, 23.

Many zoos helped in the creation of this book. The authors
would especially like to thank ZooParc de Beauval, France, Zoo
Atlanta, USA, Zoos SA, Australia, and Taronga Zoo, Australia.

Contents

When a word is printed in **bold**, you can look up its meaning in the Glossary on page 31.

Zoos

Zoos are places where people can see a lot of different animals. The animals in a zoo come from all around the world.

People can visit zoos to see animals from other parts of the world.

Zoos have special **enclosures** for each different type of animal. Some enclosures are like the animals' homes in the **wild**. They may have trees for climbing or water for swimming.

Animals such as zebras and gazelles need a lot of space to move around.

Pandas

Pandas are **mammals**. Giant pandas and red pandas are the only two kinds of panda. Giant pandas are part of the bear family. They are large and black and white.

large rounded ears

large head

eye patches

black and white fur

Giant pandas look a bit like other bears.

Red pandas make up their own animal family. They are much smaller than giant pandas. They have reddish-brown fur.

reddish-brown fur

large pointed ears

long bushy tail

eye patches

Red pandas are excellent climbers.

In the Wild

In the wild, pandas are found in countries such as China, India, and Nepal. They live in forest **habitats** in mountain areas, where fir trees and **bamboo** grow.

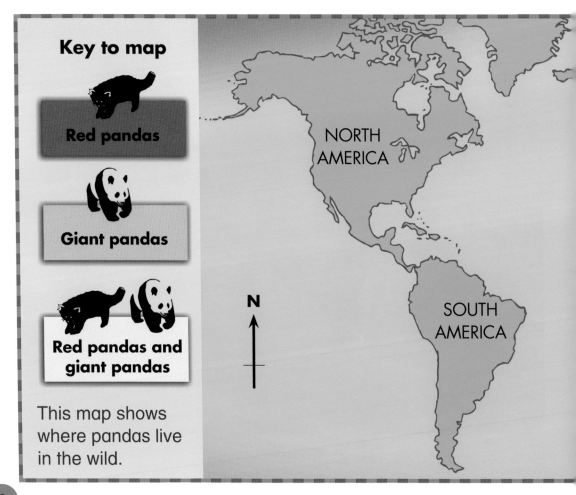

Key to map

Red pandas

Giant pandas

Red pandas and giant pandas

This map shows where pandas live in the wild.

NORTH AMERICA

SOUTH AMERICA

N

Pandas mostly eat bamboo, but they sometimes eat insects, grass, fruit, and rats. Usually, pandas live alone.

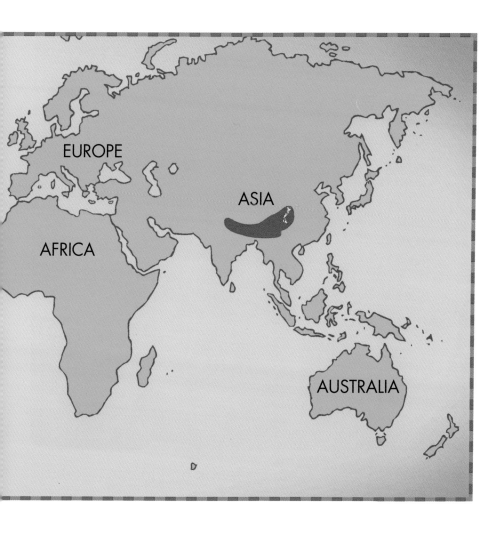

Threats to Survival

The biggest threat to the survival of pandas is the clearing of forests for towns and farms. Forests are getting smaller and farther away from each other.

Forests are cut down to make room for farms and towns.

Small forests cannot give pandas all the things they need. Pandas need large food areas and other pandas to **mate** with.

Two pandas need to mate so they can produce more pandas.

Zoo Homes

In zoos, pandas live in enclosures that look like their habitats in the wild. There are trees and rocks for shade and climbing, and a lot of bushes and bamboo plants.

trees for shade and climbing

bamboo plants

fence

Panda enclosures have a lot of plants.

Pools and streams help the pandas keep cool when the weather is hot. Enclosures for giant pandas have **dens** where the pandas can rest.

A red panda cools off under a water sprinkler during hot weather.

Zoo Food

In zoos, like in the wild, pandas eat almost nothing else besides bamboo.

Red pandas eat the leaves of bamboo plants.

Zoo Food for Red
   Pandas
bamboo leaves
fruit
biscuits

Feeding

Zoos grow their own bamboo so that they have enough to feed the pandas. Some keepers mix mashed bamboo with vitamins to make healthy bamboo cakes for the pandas.

Giant pandas spend most of their day eating bamboo.

Zoo Food for Giant Pandas

bamboo leaves and stems
sugarcane
rice gruel
hard biscuits
fruit
vegetables

Zoo Health

It can be difficult for keepers to check the health of large animals. Giant pandas are taught to cooperate during check-ups.

This zookeeper is checking a giant panda's teeth.

Zoo **veterinarians** check the health of the pandas, too. They sometimes give pandas **vaccinations**. Vaccinations protect pandas from new diseases when they are moved to other countries or areas.

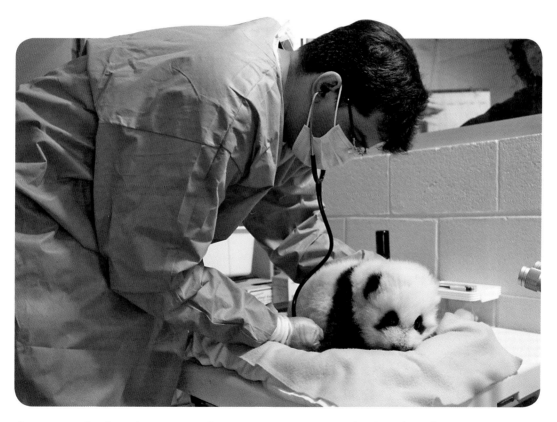

A zoo veterinarian examines a young panda to check that it is healthy.

Baby Pandas

Pandas have babies, called cubs, once each year. A mother giant panda gives birth to one or two cubs. The cubs stay with their mother for up to three years.

A newborn giant panda cub drinks its mother's milk.

Red pandas have a litter of one to four cubs.
The mother makes a nest in a hollow tree or a rock
opening. She looks after the cubs for one year.

Red panda cubs stay with their mother for about a year.

How Zoos Are Saving Pandas

Zoos help save **endangered** pandas. Beauval Zoo, in France, is helping save the red panda by raising pandas born at the zoo. This increases the number of red pandas worldwide.

A red panda eats its food safely in its enclosure at Beauval Zoo.

San Diego Zoo, in California, donates money toward research programs in China. The research is to find out how to protect giant pandas in the wild.

Money paid by visitors to zoos can help save animals in the wild.

Zoos Working Together

Zoos work together by sharing information. Some zoos find it difficult to **breed** pandas and raise cubs. Zoos that are successful share their knowledge and information with other zoos.

Zoos share information about how to breed and raise pandas.

Zoos share information about how to build the best enclosures for pandas. Adelaide Zoo, in Australia, built a new panda enclosure with information learned from other zoos.

Plans for the Giant Panda Forest at Adelaide Zoo included trees and rocky areas.

Meet Mattieu, a Panda Keeper

Mattieu works as a zookeeper at Beauval Zoo, in France.

Question	How did you become a zookeeper?
Answer	I always wanted to work with animals. I studied and found a job at a zoo.
Question	How long have you been a zookeeper?
Answer	I have been a zookeeper for four years, plus years of part-time work.

Mattieu works in the red panda enclosure.

Question	What animals have you worked with?
Answer	I have worked with eagles, big cats, apes, chimpanzees, parrots, and pandas.
Question	What do you like about your job?
Answer	I especially like the contact and involvement I have with animals.

A Day in the Life of a Zookeeper

Zookeepers have jobs they do every day. Often, a team of zookeepers work together to look after the pandas at a zoo.

8:00 a.m.
Check the panda enclosure.

10:30 a.m.
Feed the pandas.

1:00 p.m.

Check the health of the pandas.

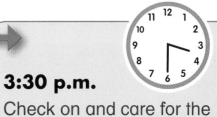

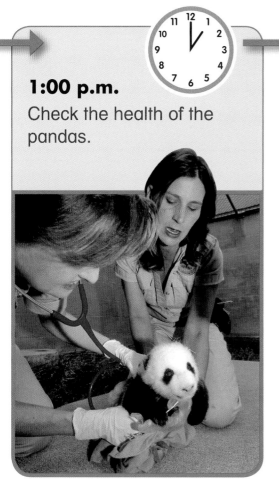

3:30 p.m.

Check on and care for the baby pandas.

Zoos Around the World

There are many zoos around the world. Ocean Park Zoo, in Hong Kong, became home to two giant pandas in 2007. Le Le and Ying Ying came from mainland China.

Le Le and Ying Ying have a special enclosure at Ocean Park Zoo.

Zurich Zoo, in Switzerland, built a high platform around its red panda enclosure. Children who visit the zoo can climb high enough to see the pandas in the trees.

Zurich Zoo has a viewing platform that children can climb.

The Importance of Zoos

Zoos do very important work. They:
- help people learn about animals
- save endangered animals and animals that are badly treated

Beijing Zoo, in China, is helping save endangered giant pandas.

Glossary

bamboo   Tall plant that has hard stems and a lot of leaves.

breed   Caring for animals so that they can produce babies.

dens   Areas where animals can hide away.

enclosures   The fenced-in areas where animals are kept in zoos.

endangered   At high risk of dying out and disappearing from Earth.

habitats   Areas in which animals are naturally found.

litter   A group of babies born together.

mammals   A group of animals, such as pandas and seals, that have fur or hair, and feed their young with their own milk.

mate   To produce babies together.

vaccinations   Medicines that prevent an animal from catching a disease.

veterinarians   Animal doctors.

wild   Natural areas, such as forests, that are untouched by humans.

Index